W9-BEH-085

SUMMARY

Where the Crawdads Sing

A Novel By
Delia Owens

Light Reads

CONTENTS

© Copyright 2019 - All rights reserved.

The content contained within this book may not be reproduced, duplicated or transmitted without direct written permission from the author or the publisher.

Under no circumstances will any blame or legal responsibility be held against the publisher, or author, for any damages, reparation, or monetary loss due to the information contained within this book. Either directly or indirectly.

Legal Notice:

This book is copyright protected. This book is only for personal use. You cannot amend, distribute, sell, use, quote or paraphrase any part, or the content within this book, without the consent of the author or publisher.

Disclaimer Notice:

This is a summary and not the original book. Please note the information contained within this document is for educational and entertainment purposes only. All effort has been executed to present accurate, up to date, and reliable, complete information. No warranties of any kind are declared or implied. Readers acknowledge that the author is not engaging in the rendering of legal, financial, medical or professional advice. The content within this book has been derived from various sources.

Please consult a licensed professional before attempting any techniques outlined in this book.

By reading this document, the reader agrees that under no circumstances is the author responsible for any losses, direct or indirect, which are incurred as a result of the use of information contained within this document, including, but not limited to, — errors, omissions, or inaccuracies.

ISBN: 9781095966020

INTRODUCTION

Congratulations on buying *Summary of Where the Crawdads Sing a Novel by Delia Owens* and thank you for doing so.

Although this is a summary of the novel in the title, this book contains every essential plot point contained in the original novel. The original novel is a New York Times best-seller, and it has stayed on the list for more than 30 weeks! It is a novel that Reece Witherspoon, herself, actually endorsed it for her book club, which led to the necessary exposure to make *Where the Crawdads Sing* shoot to the top of the charts. Clearly, you want to know what all of the excitement is about without having to drop too much cash on the novel.

Where the Crawdads Sing, the actual novel, begins with Part 1, called The Marsh, consisting of the prologue through chapter 21. Part 2, entitled The Swamp, consists of chapters 22 through 57. This summary of the novel follows the exact same chapter lineup, only telling the story in a much more concise manner, saving you time without sacrificing the plot of the novel!

There are lots of ways that you can learn about the story of the girl in the marsh, so we appreciate that you came to us first! Please enjoy this summary of a fantastic novel, and be sure to check out our other summaries available, too!

CHAPTER 1: PROLOGUE THROUGH CHAPTER 10

Part 1 – The Marsh

Prologue

The prologue is brief, yet revealing of an important plot aspect of the novel. The year is 1969. A beautiful description of the marsh is detailed, explaining how the marsh is not a swamp, but a place of light with grass and water that is home to different forms of life. However, there are places where the swamp sneaks in, filled with dark and muddy waters that have no light and no life. The body of Chase Andrews is found in the swamp beneath the old fire tower by two young boys on the morning of October 30th.

Ma

Chapter 1 begins with a backward time-jump. It is a hot, August morning in 1952. Kya is six years old and washing dishes in a basin of a rundown shack deep in the North Carolina marsh. She hears the screen door slam shut and runs for the front of the shack, wondering who had left. From the porch, she sees her mother walking away down the sandy road, wearing fake alligator heels and carrying a blue suitcase. When Kya's Ma reached the end of the lane, instead of turning and waving as normal, she just kept walking.

Kya knew this time, her mother's leaving was different. The youngest of five kids, Kya had dark hair and dark eyes. Her older brother, Jodie, tries to reassure Kya that their mother will be back, but Kya isn't convinced. When Ma doesn't return that night, Kya is even more worried. Ma had left before after fights between her and Pa, but she had always come back. This time was different. Pa comes in drunk and demanding supper. Kya's two older sisters make food, and everyone goes to bed. Ma is still not back the next day.

Jodie

It is still 1952 in Chapter 2. Weeks have gone by, and Ma hasn't returned to the shack. During this time, Kya's oldest brother and two sisters have left because of Pa's drunken rages, which usually involved physical abuse. Only Jodie, Kya, and Pa are left at the cabin. When Pa stumbles in drunk one morning, the two kids try to escape to hide in the marsh. But Pa yells for them, and Jodie sends Kya on ahead as he returns to the shack. Hours later, Jodie finds Kya. He has a swollen mouth from being hit by Pa and tells Kya that he can't stay here anymore. Jodie tells his little sister goodbye, and she watches him walk away, leaving her behind with their abusive father.

Pa doesn't come home for three days, and Kya manages to survive on turnip greens from the garden. When he does come back, he asks where everyone is, but Kya doesn't know. She goes to the beach and sees smoke coming from the direction of the shack. Running back, she finds her father burning all of her mother's belongings. A few days later, Pa gives her a dollar and change to go to town for food. He makes sure she knows that in exchange for the money, she must clean the house, gather firewood, and wash the laundry. Kya makes her first nervous trip to town for grits. There, she has her first encounter with Chase Andrews, who was a couple of years older than 6-year-old Kya. He almost runs into her on his bike. Kya never forgets that moment. Weeks go by, Ma still doesn't return, and Kya learns more about buying food, cooking, cleaning, and staying out of Pa's way.

Chase

Chapter 3 jumps forward to 1969. Steve and Benji

are the two boys that discovered the body of Chase Andrews. They go to the office of Sheriff Ed Jackson, tell him what they say, and take him to the body. The sheriff expresses concern over the fact that there are no footprints at all where Chase should have walked through the mud to climb to the top of the old fire tower.

School

Chapter 4 takes us back to 1952. The truant officer, Mrs. Culpepper, comes to the Kya's shack to take her to school because she is six. Here, we find out her name is Catherine Danielle Clark. Kya tries to go to school, but the other children make fun of her because she can't spell the word dog. Kya never returns back to school. Instead, she spends the next few weeks avoiding the truant officer until the officer gives up trying to find her. Months pass, winter comes, and Ma still doesn't come back.

Investigation

Chapter 5 takes us forward to 1969. The doctor comes to where Chase's body lies, pronouncing him dead. Deputy Joe Purdue arrives, too. Sheriff Ed explains that it looks like an accident, like Chase just fell from the fire tower, only there are absolutely no footprints. Climbing to the top of the fire tower, they find a grate open through which Chase must have fallen. They also collect hair and blood samples from a beam where Chase had hit his head on the way down. Deputy Joe says there are a lot of people who might want to kill Chase because he was quite the womanizer, despite being married.

A Boat and a Boy

Chapter 6 returns to 1952. Pa leaves for a few days to take care of some army disability business, which was their only source of income. Kya, seven now, decides to take Pa's boat out into the marsh. She gets lost and comes across Tate Walker, who used to fish with her brother, Jodie. He leads her back through the channels to her shack. We also learn a bit more about Tate when he goes back to town to help his father, a shrimp fisherman. He and his father discussed poetry, and we learn that Tate's mother and little sister are gone.

The Fishing Season

Chapter 7 stays in 1952. Kya uses her weekly money from Pa to buy gas for the boat, so he won't know she took it out. Pa comes home after 4 days. Kya had cleaned the shack, washed his bed linen, and cooked. Pa was sober for once, and they actually had a nice meal together. Kya asks him to teach her how to fish. He laughs because she is a girl, but the very next day, he takes her out in the boat to fish. Pa ends the day giving Kya his old army knapsack because he notices how she collects things from the marsh, like feathers and bird nests. The knapsack is so she will have a place to put her collection. He never gave her anything before that day.

All through the spring, Pa and Kya fish. He tells her a little bit about his family and how they used to have land and money until the Great Depression. For the first time, Pa calls Kya "hon" after they catch a big fish for dinner.

Negative Data

Chapter 8 takes place in 1969. Chase Andrews' parents identify his body. A few days later, Ed and Joe read the first of the lab reports from the coroner's office. Chase's time of death was between midnight and 2 a.m. They both assume that someone is covering up a murder because there were no footprints or fingerprints, not even Chase's, on the metal grate. When they go to the local diner to eat, someone mentions that it might have been the crazy woman who lives in the marsh who killed Chase.

Jumpin'

Chapter 9 returns to 1953. Kya goes with Pa to Jumpin's Gas and Bait marina. Jumpin' is an older black man. Pa introduces Kya and then takes her into town for her first time to eat at a restaurant. People make snide remarks, but they enjoy their dinner. Kya is outside waiting for Pa when a younger girl says hello. Kya went to reach out to her, but her mother came out and snatched the child away, telling her daughter that Kya was dirty and nasty.

Weeks go by, and Kya finds a letter from Ma in the mailbox. She leaves it on the table for Pa, and she hides. He goes into a rage and burns the letter. He leaves for a few days, comes home drunk again, and never takes Kya fishing again.

Just Grass in the Wind

Chapter 10 returns to 1969, and Ed and Joe are back at the crime scene, looking for clues. Joe thought he found a place that looked like a boat had been pulled to shore, but Ed tells him it is just from the broken grass blowing in the wind against the sand.

CHAPTER 2: CHAPTERS 11 THROUGH 20

Croker Sacks Full

Chapter 11 begins in 1956. Kya is ten. Pa comes home to the shack less and less. Weeks go by without him returning; then months. Kya resigns herself to the fact that he left her, too. He had left on foot, so she still has the boat, but she's run out of money. She collects mussels and takes them to Jumpin'. He buys them from her, and he fills up the boat's gas tank. She begins collecting mussels every day to sell, and she buys her supplies from Jumpin's store, too.

Pennies and Grits

Chapter 12 is still 1956. Kya is still alone, and she finds herself looking for the fishing boy, Tate. She sees him occasionally but never says anything.

One day, she goes to Point Beach, and she sees a group of kids on the beach. She watches them playing together, feeling lonely. She later finds out that Jumpin' can't buy mussels from her that week. She smokes fish, and he says he will sell it for her. But instead, he takes it home to his wife, Mabel, in Colored Town. She immediately wants to help, so Mabel meets Kya at Jumpin's the next day. She says that people will trade clothes and supplies for her fish, but it's really just donations from helpful people in Colored Town. The next day, there are crates of clothes and supplies waiting for her.

Feathers

Chapter 13 takes place in 1960. Kya is 14 now. She sees a boy in the forest and then finds a feather on a stump in a clearing. She knew he had left it for her. Days go by with no more feathers, and some boys sneak to her shack in the middle of the night to slap their hands on the screen door and call her Marsh girl. She finds another feather and knows the feather game is still going on.

Red Fibers

Chapter 14 finds us back in 1969. Deputy Joe tells Sheriff Ed that more lab results came in. Chase died on the ground where he was found; his injuries were consistent with the fall and hitting his head on the beam. The lab also found red fibers on his jacket that didn't come from his clothing. They decide they have to find the source of the red fibers.

The Game

Chapter 15 returns to 1960. Kya leaves a feather on the stump for her secret friend. Then, she remembers a fond memory of her Ma and sisters and herself taking the boat out for a ride and getting stuck in the mud. She finds more than a feather the next day at the stump. She finds a milk carton with vegetable seeds inside and an extra spark plug for her boat. There was also a note, but she can't read, so she just puts it away. The next day, she finds Tate in the clearing. He tells her not to be scared or run away. She thanks him for his gifts, as does he for hers. He also tells her he can teach her how to read.

Reading

Chapter 16 stays in 1960. Tired of waiting for Tate to come back to teach her to read, Kya makes a trip to Colored Town. She was looking for Jumpin', but instead hides in the weeds and watches two white boys harass Jumpin' on his way home from work. They call him hateful names and throw rocks at him, but he just keeps walking. Kya sneaks behind one of the boys and hits him in the back of the head with her knapsack of blackberry jam. Then, she goes back to her shack.

Finally, Tate returns to teach her to read. They study for hours over many days and weeks. Kya didn't talk to him much about her family or his, but she did determine that his ma had left him, too. She found herself wanting to hold his hand, but of course, she's too shy. Tate continues to teach her to read, and he teaches her basic math because she doesn't know what number comes after 29. Kya finds her Ma's family Bible, and in it, she reads her family's names and birthdates.

The book flashes back to how her pa, Jake, and her ma, Maria had met and got married. Jake did come from money before the depression, and he impressed Maria with his handsome face and big promises. When the bank foreclosed on the family land, he stole family treasures, sold them, and went to New Orleans to find Maria. He wined and dined her on the money, convincing her to marry him. He tried to go back to school but started drinking and gambling instead. They had four children within six years.

Jake went to war, and it was there that he discovered he was a coward. When his sergeant had been hurt, all the other soldiers rushed to help him except Jake. But at that moment, a mortar exploded and shattered his femur. Everyone assumed he got hurt helping save the sergeant, so he was discharged as a hero. But he knew the truth, and it haunted him forever. He packed up his family and moved to the shack in North Carolina. There, they had one more child, Kya.

Crossing the Threshold

Chapter 17 remains in 1960. Jumpin' tells Kya that

social services are looking for her. She tells Tate that they have to meet somewhere else more secluded for reading lessons. So, they start meeting at an old cabin farther in the woods – their reading cabin. After months of lessons, Kya proves to be a fast learner. Soon, she is reading much more. Tate introduces her to poetry, which she adores. When he starts his senior year, he brings her old biology books for her to study. She even invites him into her shack one cold evening.

Mabel gives Kya more supplies and lets her know that if she ever needs to talk, just to let her know. A couple of weeks later, Kya experiences intense cramping. Tate shows up, and while she tells him she thinks she is sick; he explains to her that she is probably becoming a woman. The next day, she goes to Jumpin', and he fetches Mabel for her. Kya is embarrassed but tells Mabel. Mabel hugs her and explains things to her, as well as giving her the necessary supplies for her menstrual cycle. She was almost too embarrassed to meet Tate again, but he brought her tiny cakes and acted as if nothing had happened. So, the lessons continued.

Kya finally learns that Tate's mom and little sister died in a car wreck. He blames himself because they were going to Asheville to get him a birthday gift. He finally kisses Kya gently. She asks if she is his girlfriend now. He asks if she wants to be his girlfriend. She says yes, and he agrees, kissing her again. Kya's heart is bursting with joy.

White Canoe

Chapter 18 still takes place in 1960. The lessons continue, only this time they are mixed with lots of laughter, kissing, and playfulness. Tate brings her a birthday cake to celebrate her 15th birthday, as well as gifts. He gives her all kinds of oil paints and watercolors. Tate later goes to the diner with his father. His dad is worried that he's not going to school dances. He's heard rumors about Tate and the Marsh Girl. Tate gets irritated and tells him that he's teaching her to read and that Kya is pure and innocent.

The lessons continue, and Christmas comes. Tate gives her a dictionary. Later, Kya gives him a head tuft from a male cardinal. Tate brings her leftover Christmas dinner that they share in her shack. They get close washing dishes, and they both feel a burning need, but don't act upon it. One day, in the forest, they are running and laughing. Tate gets serious. Kya gets serious. He takes her clothes off, as well as his. They kiss, and he touches her most private parts. But then he stops because she is too young for him. He doesn't want her to get pregnant.

In May, he reminds her that he's going away to college, but will come back to visit as much as possible. He leaves for college early for a job opportunity, and he promises to be back July 4th.

Something Going On

Chapter 19 returns to 1969. Joe tells Sheriff Ed that people told him Chase Andrews had something going on in the marsh. They weren't sure if it was drugs or a woman. Chase's mother is also on her way to give them information about a shell necklace.

July 4

Chapter 20 takes us to 1961. It is on the 4th of July. Kya waits for Tate. She waits for days, but he never shows up. He has left her.

CHAPTER 3: CHAPTERS 21 THROUGH 30

Coop

Chapter 21 takes place in 1961. Kya takes Tate's leaving her very hard. For an entire month after the 4th of July, she doesn't leave her shack. A cooper hawk visits her porch; she calls him Coop. She finally went to Jumpin's when she was completely out of supplies. Another month passed, and Kya started gathering items from the marsh for her collections again. The months turned into a year, then another year, and then another year. The loneliness numbed her, and she never got over Tate leaving her, especially without an explanation.

Part 2 – The Swamp

Same Tide

Chapter 22 takes us to 1965. Kya is now 19, and she is absolutely beautiful. Tall, lean, strong, tan, large eyes blacker than ever, and long, black hair. At Point Beach, she hears the sounds of young adults coming. It is the same group that she has watched for years. She hides in the weeds and trees, but one of them notices her. He doesn't give away her presence, but he turns around and smiles at her. It is Chase Andrews, handsome with black hair and blue eyes. Not wanting to admit that she wanted to see him again, Kya couldn't help herself from returning to the same beach several times, as well as visiting Jumpin's more often in hopes of seeing him again.

One day she arrives at Jumpin's, but he was nowhere to be seen. Someone touched her shoulder. It's Chase. He introduces himself and wastes no time asking her out for a picnic on his boat. She agrees.

A flashback reveals that Tate had come back to see her. He hadn't come on the 4th of July because he was offered a spot on a birding expedition at college. But 2 weeks later, he returned. He went to find her in the channels, and as he watched her, two fishermen appeared. Tate saw the wild, crazy, fearful look in her eyes as she hid from them. He realized that she would never fit into the scientific world with him –

her mind would because she was so smart about all things involving nature, but her isolation had made it impossible for her to fit into the rest of the world. He made his decision then to leave, and he never said a word to her.

The Shell

Chapter 23 takes place still in 1965. Kya meets Chase for their boat picnic. He takes her to Point Beach. There, they go for a walk, and they sit against driftwood. He plays the harmonica for her. He picks up a shell to show her, and he's surprised when she tells him all of the scientific facts about the shell, including its Latin name and why it was in the region. The shell had a single hole in it, and Chase gives it to her. They return to the boat for their picnic. After eating a large meal, they make small talk. Then, Chase kisses her, immediately laying down with her. Getting on top of Kya, she can feel him pushing against her and pulling her shirt up.

Kya freaks out and gets away from him. It was too much for her. She wasn't just going to be a booty call for him. She knew her own worth. Chase was entranced with her wildness and her beauty. He apologized and offered to take her home. But she took off running through the woods.

The Fire Tower

Chapter 24 still takes place in 1965. It has been 10 days since the picnic. She spotted Chase and his friends returning from a fishing trip. He saw her, even though she was hiding. When she returned to the beach a few minutes later, he was waiting for her alone. He apologized and took her to see the fire tower. Kya had never been, and they climbed to the top. She was amazed at how she could see the entire marsh at once. She was nervous on the steel grates, though, afraid they weren't secure. Chase apologized again, and she gave him a necklace made from rawhide that had the shell he'd given her strung on it. He put it on, then asked to see her house.

Kya reluctantly took him to her shack. He didn't seem to understand all of her collections of feathers, insects, and other items all around the shack. She also felt embarrassed that he was seeing her home. She had never felt ashamed with Tate. She asked him what he wanted with her. He admitted to wanting her at first only for sex. But he said he came on too strong, and he wanted to get to know her. Basically, they would just take it one day at a time.

A Visit from Patti Love

Chapter 25 brings up back to 1969. Patti Love, Chase's mom, shows up at the sheriff's office. She says she knows his death wasn't an accident, he would have never just fallen off the fire tower. She also tells Ed and Joe that Chase had a shell necklace that he had worn for years. She says he was wearing it the night he died because he had come to her home for dinner. He never took the necklace off, but it wasn't on his body when they identified it. She found out from the coroner that there was no necklace. Patti is sure that whoever killed him took the necklace.

Reluctantly, she admits that the Marsh Girl had made it for him, that Chase had been seeing her for a while until Chase married another girl, Pearl. Patti believes that Kya killed Chase out of spite for him leaving her. After Patti leaves, Joe and Ed decide to pay Kya a visit the next day, but first, they have to make sure the necklace wasn't anywhere around the fire tower, which it wasn't.

When they arrive at Kya's home the next day, she's nowhere to be found.

The Boat Ashore

Chapter 26 goes back to 1965. Chase and Kya are spending time together every day. She paints grasses, and he doesn't understand the beauty. After he leaves, she sees Tate in the marsh. She hides from him and rows away. Chase and Kya spend lots of time together over the next few weeks. He finally asks permission to kiss her, and she says yes. Then, they just cuddle.

A few days later, Tate is racing to the shack to find Kya. He's realized that he loves her, that he was wrong to just leave her like that, and that he doesn't want to live without her. He sees her boat and realizes that Chase's boat is coming towards her. He watches them circle each other until they are close enough to touch hands and share a kiss. He knew Chase couldn't be trusted, but he feels that he can't say anything to Kya because he had been the one to leave her.

A few days later, Kya gets tired of waiting for Chase to show up, so she goes to the reading cabin for three days. When Chase can't find her for three days, he starts making specific plans with her for his visits, so that she doesn't have to wait for him anymore. Kya dreams of a life with him, of meeting his family and making friends with his friends. One day, Chase takes her swimming. He watches her take her clothes off, pulls her down onto a towel, and starts touching her. She wants him but gets scared. Chase says they have waited long enough, but Kya isn't ready. He tells her he cares for her, and he doesn't know why they are waiting.

He says he is falling in love with her. Kya doesn't know what to think or how to feel. He agrees to wait. The next day, Kya runs into his parents in town. She thinks they know about her, but they avoid her like the plague. She asks Chase if she would meet them soon. He avoids looking at her but says yes. He tells her they know about her. Weeks go by, and Kya still resists having sex with Chase. They fooled around, but nothing more, even though the townsfolk gossiped about them.

Out Hog Mountain Road

Chapter 27 takes place in 1966. Chase talks to Kya

about marrying her, about building her a house. Then he invites her on an out-of-town trip with him to Asheville. He says they will stay the night in a motel. She realizes what the trip is really about, but agrees to go. On the trip, she sees the mountains for the first time, as well as the big city. Chase takes her to a cheap motel and told her it was time. She agreed. After all, he said he was going to marry her. It was a painful experience, and it lacked the tenderness they had shared all these months.

Weeks later, sex between the two of them had become a normal part of their routine, but Kya was always left unsatisfied. She asked if she could go to his home for Christmas dinner, but Chase made numerous excuses about why she wouldn't enjoy it. He said all that mattered was their time together in the shack. Kya was alone on Christmas again.

Four days later, Chase hadn't come back, and Kya was annoyed. She heard a boat and thought it was him. But it was Tate. Angry, Kya threw rocks at him and told him to leave her lagoon. Tate was apologetic and tried to explain that he just wanted to explain and get her forgiveness. He also told her that she didn't know Chase was seeing other women in town. They argued, but Kya finally calmed down and let Tate come in her shack to see her collections.

He was in awe. He offered to take some of her samples to a publisher, and she agreed. He asked her forgiveness, but she doesn't know how to give it. She can't get his words about Chase out of her head. Finally, Chase shows up a week later.

The Shrimper

Chapter 28 brings us to 1969. Ed and Joe go to the Dog-Gone, a beer joint, to listen for gossip about the case. Hal Miller, a shrimper, talks to Ed alone. He tells him that the night Chase died, as the shrimp boat was coming back to shore, he and another crewmember case the Marsh Girl in her boat coming out of the bay, headed in the direction of the Fire Tower.

Seaweed

Chapter 29 goes back to 1967. Chase came to Kya's shack a lot, spending the night at least once a week. In March, Kya goes to town to get ingredients to make Chase a birthday cake. She runs right into Chase and all of his friends on the pier in town. He has his arm around a blond girl but drops it when he sees Kya. He introduces them, then Kya goes on her way, and he goes with his friends. She gets the ingredients for the cake, and can't get the image of his arm around the girl out of her head. She buys a paper to read about a new lab being built.

At home again, she reads the article about the lab. As she turns the page to continue reading, she is faced with a picture of Chase and the blond girl – it's an engagement announcement. Chase is marrying the other girl, Pearl. Kya is reeling, leaves the shack, and doesn't come out of the woods when Chase arrives. She knows he will see the paper on the table, and he will know that she knows.

The Rips

Chapter 30 still takes place in 1967. Kya is angry and heads out into the angry ocean waters. She understands that Chase only talked about marriage to get her into bed. The waters are rough, and she is soaked and scared. She finally lands on a small sand bar. She gathers herself, along with some very rare shells, and makes her way back home.

CHAPTER 4: CHAPTERS 31 THROUGH 40

A Book

Chapter 31 finds us in 1968. Kya is 22 now and checking the mailbox every day. She finally gets what she is waiting for – a copy of her book, The Sea Shells of the Eastern Seaboard. Tate had given the samples to a publisher, and Kya had been in touch with the publisher. They wanted her book published immediately, and they paid her $5,000 in advance. The book was beautiful, and it would bring in royalties every 6 months. Kya wrote Tate a thank you note and told him to come by for a copy of the book.

Kya hires a handy-man, and he installs electricity, running water, a water heater, and a new bathroom. She also gets a new fridge and range but keeps her wood stove. New cabinets and furniture are next – Kya finally has a real bed. When she hears that developers are coming to the marsh, she goes to the county clerk to find out if she owns the land she lives on. She does and only has to pay $800 for forty years of back taxes because her land is considered waste-land. She is the proud owner of 310 acres of marshland.

Tate comes over, and she gives him her book. He has her sign it. She writes "To the Feather Boy, Thank you, From the Marsh Girl." They both know they still have feelings, but Kya is too afraid to trust him again. Later, Kya goes to Jumpin's and gives him a copy of her book. She tells him she is okay now. He is very proud of her and displays her book in his store window the way a proud daddy would have done.

Alibi

Chapter 32 is back in 1969 again. Jo has news for Ed. He has been to Jumpin's and Kya has a strong alibi. Both Jumpin' and Tate say that she was in Greenville for two nights. One of those nights was the night Chase dies. She was in Greenville to meet with her editor. Joe also says that Tate told him he was the one who told her how to get a bus ticket, and that he had known her for years and taught her to read. Later, Pansy Price from the five and dime store comes in and says that she was Kya leave on the bus on October 28 and come back on the 30th. She reinforces Kya's alibi.

Ed and Joe aren't convinced. They decide to find out if there is a night bus from Greenville to Barkley Cove. There was, which means Kya could have left in the day, returned under the cover of darkness, killed Chase, and left again.

The Scar

Chapter 33 takes us to 1968. Someone pulls up to the shack in a red truck. The man approaches, and Kya realizes it is Jodie. She flashes back to the memory of the Easter before Ma left. There was a big fight between Ma and Pa and Jodie. Pa hit Ma with a fire poker, making her chest bleed. Jodie stepped in, and Pa laid him out on the floor by hitting him across the face with the poker. Ma and Kya hid in the weeds until it was safe to come out. Ma had stitched up Jodie's face, but there was still a huge scar. Kya realizes that she had blocked that memory out, and she now understood a little more about why Ma had left.

Kya is thrilled to see Jodie. He had seen her book, and he had come to find her. Jodie is in the army. He apologizes for not taking Kya with him when he left. She tells him about how Pa eventually left her, too. Kya doesn't blame Jodie for leaving, so she forgives him. He doesn't know where the rest of their siblings are, and he finally tells Kya that he found out their Ma died two years ago. Kya is devastated. Ma's sister, Rosemary, had finally tracked Jodie down to tell him the whole story.

When Ma had moved to the shack, she kept in touch with her family through letters. She wrote about the abuse often. When she finally showed up back at her family home one day, she was in a bad mental state. She didn't speak. It was almost a year before

Ma became hysterical because she had left her children behind. That was when she wrote the letter young Kya had found, and Pa had burned. The letter asked him to let her come get her kids. But Pa had written back that if she ever showed up to get the kids, he would beat them until they were unrecognizable.

Ma never came to get them because she feared if she did, he would hurt or even kill the children. She was miserable, sad, and broken. She developed leukemia and refused treatment, so it eventually killed her. Then Jodie took Kya to his truck and showed her numerous paintings Ma had painted over the years. The paintings were pictures of the children when they were small. There was even a painting of a toddler Kya and Tate looking at butterflies.

Jodie stayed for a few days, and she told him about Tate. He suggested that she give Tate another chance, but she says she can't trust him. Jodie leaves her his address and phone number, and Kya finally has at least one person she can call family.

Search the Shack

Chapter 34 takes us back to 1969. Ed and Joe show up at Kya's shack, but she's not there. They have a warrant, go inside, and start searching. The only thing they find is a red wool hat hanging on a hook. They take it to see if the fibers match the ones found on Chase's body.

The Compass

Chapter 35 takes place in 1969. Kya's second book about seacoast birds hits the shelves. She goes to the old clearing with the stump and finds a gift from Tate – a compass. She keeps it in her knapsack. She knows she still loves him, but she just can't bring herself to trust him again.

To Trap a Fox

Chapter 36 takes place in 1969. Joe tells Sheriff Ed that the fibers from Chase's coat match exactly to the fibers of the red hat found at Kya's cabin. They decide they need to set a trap to finally find Kya. On December 15, Rodney Horn comes to the office. He tells them about an event that happened on August 30th when he and a friend were fishing. Ed and Joe decide they now have a motive.

Gray Sharks

Chapter 37 still takes place in 1969. Kya knew the sheriff was looking for her. She goes to Jumpin's, and he tries to signal her that it's not safe. Suddenly, she is surrounded by boats. She tries to escape to sea, but her efforts in her small boat are futile. Kya is placed under arrest for the murder of Chase Andrews.

Sunday Justice

Chapter 38 takes place in 1970. Kya is in court. She

has been in jail for two months. She is miserable. She has a good attorney who came out of retirement to represent her. His name is Tom Milton. It took a couple of visits for Kya to trust him, but he wanted to help her. She refused to talk about the night of Chase's death. In court, Sunday Justice is the courtroom cat. Kya enjoys the cat. She misses the marsh desperately. Tom points out the different people in the courtroom, like the bailiff, and explains what everyone is doing. The judge comes in and denies Tom's request for a change of venue. The jury selection process begins. The death penalty is a possible punishment if Kya is convicted. The jury winds up being 7 women and 5 men.

Chase by Chance

Chapter 39 takes place in 1969 again. Kya is looking for rare mushrooms for another book. She runs unexpectedly into Chase. She asks him to leave, but he refuses. He has been drinking. He says he is sorry, but she should have known they could never get married. He says he always cared about her, and he wants to go back to the way things were, the two of them being together in the marsh at the shack.

Chase gets aggressive with her, and he tries to rape her. He knocks her down, and Kya fights back, yelling angry words. He hits her with his fist, pulling her shorts and panties down. He rolls her over, and she somehow finds the strength to get up and push him off of her. She kicks him in the groin and the back several times. She rushes to her boat, trying to pull her clothes back on. She cussed and yelled as she tried to start her motor. Finally pulling away, she gets her clothes pulled up, and sees a fishing boat nearby with two men just staring at her.

Cypress Cove

Chapter 40 puts us back in 1970. The trial is underway. The prosecution, Eric, calls Rodney Horn to the stand. Rodney tells his story. The day he and his friend were fishing was the day that they saw Kya half naked, scared, and escaping from Chase. They had heard her hollering, and they motored over to see if she was in trouble. They saw her kicking Chase, and Rodney testifies that they heard Kya tell Chase to leave her alone, and if he bothers her again, she will kill him. Tom cross-examines, having Rodney admit that it was possible Kya was defending herself from Chase. Eric reiterates that Kya was very mad and threatened to kill Chase. Rodney is done testifying.

CHAPTER 5: CHAPTERS 41 THROUGH 50

A Small Herd

Chapter 41 takes us back to 1969. Kya is racing away from Chase, afraid that he will follow her. He had said that she was his. But she knew she couldn't tell anyone because no one would believe her. They would say she wasn't behaving like a lady. She hides in the reading cabin for the night. She awakens with a bruised and battered face from Chase hitting her. She returns to the shack and spends her days in the marsh, avoiding places Chase knew about. Her body hurts from their wrestling match when he tried to rape her. Her face is still swollen and bruised.

A Cell

Chapter 42 brings us to 1970. Kya is sitting in her jail

cell. She tries so hard to see out of her cell window because she misses the marsh so much. She feels like a caged animal. She could hear the talk between two other inmates – they were talking about her. She ignores them; she doesn't fear death. She fears the thought of dying at the will of someone else, of someone else planning her death, being in control of it.

A Microscope

Chapter 43 goes back to 1969. It has been over a week since Chase's attack. Kya is at her beach, holding a letter from her editor. She's been invited to Greenville because he wants to meet her. She's uncertain what to do. As she motors around the marsh, she sees Tate. She tries to avoid him because her face is still bruised, but he sees her, calling her over to see his new microscope. Kya gets on his boat, keeping the left side of her face hidden from Tate's view. She views a drop of water under the microscope, and she's in awe over the living organisms inside the drop of water.

Tate senses that Kya is acting even more guarded than usual. He makes her a cup of coffee, and he sees her bruised face. Tate asks her what happened, but Kya says she ran into a door in the middle of the night. He knows she is lying, but he changes the subject because he doesn't want her to leave. They talk about the book of mushrooms she is working on. She tells him about the invitation to Greenville.

Tate urges her to go, telling her how to buy a bus ticket, and letting her know Jumpin' has the bus schedule at his store.

Kya leaves, and Tate tells her it's cold. He tosses her his red ski cap. She tosses it back. They laugh as they playfully throw the hat back and forth between them. Kya leaves, telling herself that she will not fall for Tate again because he will hurt her. She stops at the beach on the way home to feed the gulls. She hears the roar of Chase's boat, and she hides from him. Kya knew he would come back because he would want revenge for her kicking him. Kya knows that Chase is not going to just forget about her and the fight – he's not going to let it go. She wonders to herself who it is that decides it is the time to die.

Cell Mate

Chapter 44 leads us back to 1970, and Kya is still in her cell. She's thinking about her loneliness, about how if everyone hadn't left her, none of this would be happening. She realizes that every time she depends on someone, she gets hurt. Kya believes the only person she can trust is herself. Everyone always abandons her, so she will always be alone, and she will always survive alone. The guard tells Kya that her lawyer is here to see her.

Tom starts discussing a plea agreement. He explains that if she says she is guilty of manslaughter, she gets a lower sentence, maybe six years of time in prison. Kya refuses to say she is guilty, and she refuses to go to prison. She tells Tom to get her out of jail, one way or another. She goes back to her cell, and Sunday Justice, the courtroom cat, slinks in between the bars, sleeping all through the night with her. Kya loves the feeling of simply being accepted for herself. In the morning, Kya asks the guard to please let Sunday Justice in again that night, so he does, and the cat sleeps with her again. With the cat, she is finally able to get some actual peaceful sleep for once during her time in jail.

The next day, Tate comes to visit her. She agrees to see him, and as they talk, he tells her that he sits right behind her in the courtroom. He talks about what they will do when she gets out of jail. Kya tells Tate to forget about her, that she will never fit in with the people in his world. She believes she is meant to just be alone. She talks about how long she wanted friends and a family, but everyone always left her. She is strong enough now to take care of herself, so she doesn't need anyone else. It is just better that way. Tate tells her that he feeds her gulls for her while she is gone.

Red Cap

Chapter 45 begins in 1970. Kya is back in court the day after Tate comes to visit her. She sees Jumpin' and Mabel sitting right behind her. The coroner is called to the stand. He testifies that Chase died between midnight and 2 in the morning from injuries sustained during a fall. He also says that there were no drugs or alcohol in his system that might have led to an accidental fall. The prosecutor discusses how Chase had to have fallen backward because his head injury was on the back of his head. The coroner says the injury is consistent with a backward fall. The prosecutor makes it clear that he believes if Chase had fallen accidentally, he would have fallen forward, hitting the front of his head. A backward fall could mean that he was pushed.

The prosecutor brings up the red fibers on Chase's jacket and the matching red fibers from the hat found at Kya's cabin. Tom Milton cross-examines the coroner, getting him to admit that while Chase could have been pushed backward, there were no injuries suggesting that he was pushed. He also pressed the fact that even though the fibers belonged to Kya's hat, since she and Chase had spent so much time together over the years, the fibers could have been on the jacket for a long time. The coroner confirms all of it. The fibers could have been there for a day or a year or longer; there was no way to know. Recessing for lunch finds Kya back in the cell. She ponders calling Jodie, but she doesn't know what to say to him.

King of the World

Chapter 46 goes back to 1969. Kya needs to go to Jumpin's to get the bus schedule. She knows the bruise is still on her face, but it is a faint yellow now, so she thinks she is safe to go out in public again. But

Jumpin' notices right away, and he makes her tell him what happened. He already knew before she said his name that the culprit was Chase. Jumpin' is very upset because he loves Kya like a child of his own. But she makes him promise not to tell anyone because no one will believe her. Jumpin' makes her promise to check in about every day so that he knows she is okay, and that Chase hasn't come back to finish her off.

The Expert

Chapter 47 takes us right back to 1970 in the courtroom. Sheriff Ed is on the stand. He explains why he thinks Chase was murdered – there were no footprints at all or fingerprints. He thinks the evidence was destroyed on purpose. Tom cross-examines Ed. He makes him admit that the rising water of the tide could have easily washed away any tracks. He makes Ed admit that since there were no fingerprints found, that means Kya's fingerprints weren't found anywhere, as well as none of her long hair is found. Tom stresses that there is no proof that Kya was at the fire tower the night Chase died. He also reminds the sheriff that he had written a letter to the Forest Service asking for them to close the fire tower because the grates were constantly being left open by kids, and someone could get hurt or die. This letter was written only 3 months before Chase's death.

A Trip

Chapter 48 jumps back to 1969. Kya lets Jumpin' know she is going to Greenville. She lets him know when she returns two days later. Jumpin' informs Kya about Chase's death. Kya is in shock. Jumpin' lets her know that people in the town are talking about her because Chase's necklace was missing, and everyone knew that Chase and Kya had spent a lot of time together during their affair. Jumpin' is glad that Kya was in Greenville when Chase died, or it would have been pinned on Kya.

Disguises

Chapter 49 takes us back to the courtroom in 1970. The prosecutor has called a bus driver to the stand. Larry Price testifies that he was the one driving the bus from Greenville to Barkley Cove the night that Chase Andrews had died. He says that he did not see Kya, but he saw a slim, tall man with a baseball cap that could have been Kya in disguise. In cross-examination, Tom gets Larry to admit that all he really knows is - there wasn't a woman on the bus that night, and there was a tall, slim man, but Larry couldn't see his face. Larry also mentions that the bus was late that night. The prosecutor calls another bus driver to the stand, the one that drove the night back from Barkley Cove to Greenville. This driver testified that he didn't see Kya on the bus, only an older woman who could have been Kya in disguise. He couldn't be certain.

The Journal

Chapter 50 remains in 1970. Kya walks into the courtroom to see Tate, Mabel, Jumpin', and Jodie. She is surprised but happy to see her brother. The prosecutor calls Chase's mom to the stand, Patti Love. She talks about the necklace and how Chase never took it off. She is also shown a private journal that Kya had made for and given to Chase. It had paintings of their various memories inside, such as a painting of Chase playing the harmonica like on their first picnic date. Patti says that she found the journal in Chase's room one day, and he was forced to tell her that he was seeing Kya. Another picture is pointed out – one of Kya and Chase on the fire tower. In the painting, Kya is giving Chase the shell necklace no one can find. Tom had no cross-examination questions for her.

CHAPTER 6: CHAPTERS 51 THROUGH 57

Waning Moon

Chapter 51 takes place still in 1970 in the court-room at Kya's murder trial. Hal Miller is called to the stand. He testifies that he was coming in on a shrimp boat around 1:45 in the morning of October 30, 1969. He says that he and a crewmate saw Kya in her boat heading in the direction of the fire tower. He is positive it was her because he's seen her a lot over the years in her boat. When Tom cross-exam-ines him, Hal admits that the moon was not out yet, so it was really dark. He says he wasn't close enough to see what Kya was wearing. Tom makes a point that Hal was about 60 yards away, so how could he know it was Kya? Hal says he could tell it was her by the slim, tall shape, but no, he guesses he wasn't

100% sure.

Three Mountains Motel

Chapter 52 is still in 1970 at the murder trial. The prosecution rests, so Tom calls Mrs. Singletary from the Piggly Wiggly to the stand. She testifies that she saw Kya board the bus on the afternoon of October 28th, and she saw her get off the bus on the afternoon of October 30th. Other cashiers saw her, too. The prosecution, Eric, doesn't have any questions, and he makes a point of saying that a lot of the defense witnesses are going to say the same thing – they saw Kya board the bus and get off the bus two days later. He asks that the record note that he accepts this as fact, meaning Tom doesn't get to call a lot of his witnesses to the stand, which upsets him because he needs the jury to believe Kya's alibi of being out of town.

Tom calls Lang Furlough to the stand. He runs the Three Mountains Motel in Greenville. He testifies that he worked the desk all night on October 29th, and he never saw Kya leave her room. Eric cross-examines, and Mr. Furlough admits that he left the desk several times, enough that there was a chance that Kya left her room without him seeing her.

After the recess for lunch, Tate's father, Scupper, shows up at court to be there for Tate. He realizes that he was just as guilty as everyone else of judging Kya without knowing her story of hardship – and she had lived a hard life as an abandoned child. Tom calls Robert Foster to the stand. He is the editor Kya met in Greenville. He recalls the times he took Kya to dinner and back to her room, watching her go inside. He tells the court when he picked her up for breakfast, too.

Eric cross-examines and asks why Kya stayed in the rather lackluster Three Mountains Motel instead of the swanky hotel where Mr. Foster stayed. Mr. Foster testifies that she was offered the better hotel, but insisted on staying at the shabby motel. Eric makes the point that she could have easily walked to the bus station, boarded a bus in the middle of the night, came back, and no one would have noticed, implying that she wanted to stay in the motel, so she could murder Chase. Tom redirects and talks about how shy and isolated Kya was, making a point that for someone like her, it made sense that she would want to stay in a small motel away from the crowds of people. It also made sense that she would choose that motel because she didn't have a car, and she could walk to it without using public transportation, which she knew nothing about.

Tom calls the sheriff back to the stand. He goes over the timeline of how long it would take Kya to bus back to town, motor out to the fire tower, and get back to town to catch the bus back to Greenville. She would need at least a little over an hour. Since the bus to town was late, there simply wasn't enough time for her to kill Chase and catch the bus back to Greenville. The sheriff gives a few other theories trying to explain the time difference, such as if she jogged or if the currents were fast. But Sheriff Ed has no proof of anything, so it is all just theory.

Missing Link

Chapter 53, still 1970, brings us to the last witness Tom has for Kya. He calls Tim O'Neal to the stand. Tim is the captain of the shrimp boat that Hal works for, and he testifies that he, too, saw the boat, but that it was much too dark to say for sure if it was Kya's boat, much less even Kya. The defense rests. Closing arguments consist of Eric talking about Kya telling Chase she would kill him in the marsh the day the fishermen heard them arguing. He talks about the red fibers matching. He says they must convict her.

Tom gets to the point. He says that the town has always called Kya the Marsh Girl, teasing her that she was the missing link between man and ape and that they have always passed judgment on her when she was just a small child who had been abandoned in the marsh. None of the townspeople had helped her, only Jumpin' and his family and friends helped her. Tom says that the jury must judge Kya only on the facts of the case, which include her solid alibi on the night of the murder. There is also no evidence tying her to the crime scene other than red fibers that could have easily been on Chase's coat for days or years. He says it is time for the town to finally be fair to the Marsh Girl.

Vice Versa

Chapter 54 takes place still in 1970. Everyone is waiting for the jury to bring back a verdict. Kya has to wait alone in her cell. Over the course of a few hours, the jury asks to see different parts of the testimony, which could be a good or bad sign. Around 4 in the afternoon, the jury has a verdict. No one knows if it is a good or bad sign. The courtroom is packed, spilling over into the halls and the streets.

The jury hands the bailiff the paper with their verdict. He gives it to the judge. The judge hands it to the court reporter. Tate is frustrated and asks that someone just read it. The jury finds Miss Catherine Danielle Clark, also known as Kya, not guilty of the murder of Chase Andrews. The court erupts. Many are upset with the verdict. Kya is in shock. The people eventually go their separate ways, back to their lives outside of the courtroom. Jodie offers to take Kya home. She is finally free.

Grass Flowers

Chapter 55 picks right up in 1970 when Jodie takes Kya home. She goes first to see her gulls. She and Jodie talk about how she has always been alone her whole life, she just hopes people now will leave her alone completely. Kya says it shouldn't take an acquittal to be accepted by a community. She says she never hated anyone – they all hated her. They teased her, laughed at her, left her, attacked her, so she just learned how to live without anyone. Without Ma, Pa, and without Jodie. She leaves the cabin in exhaustion, hiding in the forest until Jodie finally leaves.

The next day, Kya is in her boat, and she sees Tate. Before she can get to him, the sheriff and deputy pull up on an airboat. She sees them talking to Tate, sees him hang his head, shoulders drooping. He reaches up to the deputy, who pulls him aboard the airboat and then drives Tate's boat behind them out of the marsh. Kya is worried, wondering if Tate had been arrested. She realizes that all of these years in the marsh, she survived each day because she hoped to catch even a glimpse of Tate. She loves him, and now he may be in trouble. She rushes to Jumpin's to find out what's going on.

The Night Heron

Chapter 56 – the year is still 1970, and people are leaving the cemetery where Tate's dad was laid to rest. That is why the sheriff came to the marsh to find him – to tell him Scupper was gone. Tate feels guilty that he's been so consumed with Kya, he didn't spend time with his dad. But he also knows that his dad understood the meaning of love. Tate visits his father's grave, along with his mother's and sister's graves. Then, he goes to the marsh to find Kya. Upon reaching her cabin, he gets out, and Kya comes out. She comes to him, he holds her and tells her he loves her. She tells him that she has always loved him, even when she was a child and doesn't even remember him, she already loved him.

The Firefly

Chapter 57 takes place over the course of many years. Tate and Kya spend their first night together on the beach. Tate moves in with her the very next day. They don't get officially married because Kya says they are married like the geese. Tate builds her a lab and a studio. They also add a bedroom to the shack, a larger living room, and a bigger bathroom. Kya wants the kitchen to remain the same – it has always reminded her of Ma. She also doesn't let the outside of the cabin get painted because she says it looks more real the way it is.

Jodie and his wife come to visit. Kya never returns to Barkley Cove, instead of living her life with Tate, both of them simply loving each other and their time together. The townspeople gossiped about the murder and Kya until both became town legends. One day, Tate tells Kya that Jumpin' died. Kya is heartbroken because while people she loved had always left her, they did it by choice. Jumpin' was her first experience with a loss like this, one that wasn't by choice. She went to visit Mabel, who tells her that Jumpin' loved her like a daughter, and Kya says Jumpin' was her Pa. Finally, Kya is able to forgive her Ma for leaving.

Time moves on, and Jodie and his wife often visit with their children. The cabin was filled with love and laughter and family. Barkley Cove grows fast over the years, becoming a tourist attraction. Tate works for the lab and Kya publishes 7 more books. They never had a child, although they wanted one and tried. It just wasn't meant to be, so they loved each other even more. Kya realizes that her connection isn't with a family so much as it is with the earth. She is born of Mother Earth.

When Kya is 64, Tate goes to find her after she doesn't come back from collecting in the marsh. He finds her lying down in her boat, but when he calls her name, she doesn't answer. Kya has passed away peacefully in her favorite place in the world – the marsh. Tate is shattered. He gets permission to bury her under an oak tree on her land near the sea. The entire town came to the services for Kya. Tate inscribes on her headstone her legal name, Kya, and The Marsh Girl – because it was no longer an insult, but a testament to the fact that Kya was a legend.

Tate goes to the shack, where he will live out the rest of his life. In the kitchen, he notices that the stack of wood is low – low enough that he sees something underneath. It is a trapdoor to a small compartment that held a box full of poems. Amanda Hamilton had written the poems, and many were published in local publications. He also finds handwritten poems by Kya, realizing that Kya was actually Amanda Hamilton. One poem stands out to him. It is called *The Firefly*.

The poem talks about how easy it was to lure "him," how it took only a final touch and a trap and down "he" falls, how his eyes never left hers, and that there was finally an end. Tate knew what he would find next. He found the shell necklace. The poem was Kya's confession to killing Chase. Tate burned everything, then he threw the shell back out to sea. Kya's secrets would never be found out. When he returns to the shack, he looks back at the fireflies in the distance, way out where the crawdads sing.

CONCLUSION

Thank you for making it through to the end of *Summary of Where the Crawdads Sing a Novel by Delia Owens*, let's hope it was exactly what you were searching for when you decided you wanted to know more about this best-selling novel.

Clearly, the novel is a huge success, and this summary has shown you why. The story of a young girl abandoned in the marshes with no one to take care of her, but herself – that is a true story. The added appeal of the murder plot in addition to Kya's life story only makes this novel better. Hopefully, you were pleased with this summary of the novel, as we tried hard to include as much information as possible without forcing you to read the actual novel.

We hope that you enjoyed every second of this summary eBook. The actual novel has found great success in the literary world, and now, you can join in on the next discussion about *Where the Crawdads Sing*, and you will know that you have all of the necessary information needed to talk about this amazing novel. Finally, if you found this book useful in any way, if it fulfilled your need to know what all the hype is surrounding the novel without actually having to read the novel, a review on Amazon is always appreciated!

55655274R00035

Made in the USA
Middletown, DE
17 July 2019